Growing
Apples
and
Pumpkins

by Amy and Richard Hutchings
Photographs by Richard Hutchings

Cartwheel
·B·O·O·K·S·® SCHOLASTIC INC.

New York Toronto London Auckland Sydney
Mexico City New Delhi Hong Kong

This book is a tribute to Scott and Lisa Applegate,
as well as their three wonderful children.
We appreciate their hard work at Battlecreek Orchards to bring
us fresh juicy apples and pumpkins each year.
— A.H., R.H.

ISBN 0-439-22352-0

Text copyright © 2001 by Amy and Richard Hutchings.
Illustrations copyright © 2001 by Richard Hutchings.
All rights reserved. Published by Scholastic Inc.
SCHOLASTIC, CARTWHEEL BOOKS, and associated logos
are trademarks and/or registered trademarks of Scholastic Inc.

Library of Congress Cataloging-in-Publication Data

Hutchings, Amy.
    Growing apples and pumpkins / by Amy and Richard Hutchings; photographs by Richard Hutchings.
    p. cm.
    ISBN 0-439-22352-0
    1. Apples—Juvenile literature. [1. Apples. 2. Pumpkins.]
    I. Hutchings, Richard. II. Title.
    SB363.H88 2001
    634'.11—dc21
                                                                    00-06789
12 11 10 9 8 7 6 5 4   08 09 10 11 12

Printed in the U.S.A.
First printing, October 2001

Meet farmer Scott Applegate, his wife Lisa, and their sons Kyle and Mitchell. Soon they'll welcome a new baby to the family!

Scott and his family grow apples and pumpkins on a farm in New Jersey.

It's the end of February, and the snow is gone. Mitchell and his mom look at buds on the apple trees, all shut tight from the cold winter. By springtime the buds will open into blossoms. Later they will grow into apples.

Scott checks out the farm, with Kyle and Mitchell along for the ride. Winter is almost over, and soon Scott can plant new young apple trees called *saplings*.

By the middle of March it's time to plant the new trees. Scott gets a lot of help from farm workers Carlos and José.

Scott drives his tractor over the fields. At the back of the tractor is a *tree planter* that plows a ditch in the soil. Carlos sits on the tree planter and places a sapling in the ditch about every twelve feet.

After the small tree is put into the ditch, José straightens the tree and packs the moist soil around it.

When the trees are firmly planted, they're ready for *pruning*. Scott cuts them back about six inches.

Now he has to take care of the older trees. Scott prunes the weak limbs so that only the strong limbs will be left to grow. He places *spreaders* between the branches of the younger of these trees, forcing them to grow horizontally. This way a lot of sunlight can reach the branches and more fruit will grow. Scott also wraps the tree trunks with *tree guards* to keep animals from eating the bark and hurting his trees.

April brings good news. Lisa has a baby girl, Jessica.

May brings warmer, longer days and the apple trees have begun to flower. Kyle and Mitchell love to play in the flowering orchard with their friend Maggie.

Scott has a beekeeper move beehives into the orchard. Bees are great helpers in the orchard. These insects carry flower pollen from one tree to another, making more flowers bloom and allowing more apples to grow.

The flowers grow in groups of five. The first flower to bloom is called the *king blossom*. The king blossom has the best chance of growing into an apple. Scott uses a *selective spray* to knock off the other blossoms. This is called *thinning*. Fewer apples will grow but those that do will be bigger and more colorful. Also, the tree limbs won't break from the weight of too many apples.

The apples have just started to form when Scott gets the ground ready for planting pumpkins.

First, he must turn over the soil. He hooks up a *disk harrow* to his tractor. The strong metal disks dig into the dirt and turn it around, bringing the soil from the bottom up to the top. This helps to loosen the soil so that as the plants grow, their roots will spread more easily.

Next, Scott uses a *spreader* to add fertilizer containing *nutrients* to the soil.

On a sunny day in June, Scott prepares to plant the pumpkin seeds. Mitchell watches closely as Scott smoothes over the loosened soil with a *spring-toothed harrow*. This rakes the soil and makes it even.

Then Scott fills the *planter* with seeds. The planter crosses back and forth over the field and digs trenches two inches deep. About every three to four feet, it drops a seed into a trench, then covers it with dirt.

Every year Scott plants extra large pumpkins called Atlantic Dill Giants. This year, Mitchell gets to plant one of his own. Mitchell won't use the planter. He wants to plant his seed by hand.

The sun, rain, and nutrients in the soil give the seeds what they need to open and grow. In two weeks — presto! The seeds have sprouted.

The pumpkin plants grow really fast. By the middle of July, they start to flower. There are "female" flowers and "male" flowers. The "females" are the only ones that can become pumpkins. Scott brings the bees in again to help grow more pumpkins.

Meanwhile, Kyle and his friend Hector check on the apples.

During July, the apples and pumpkins continue to grow. The boys have fun playing baseball and football in the orchards.

Mitchell looks in on his pumpkin. Like everything else in the field, it's getting bigger.

By August, the apples are
starting to change colors.
Scott grows different kinds
of apples. Rome Beauties
and Red Delicious apples
change from green to red.
The Golden Delicious apples
change from green to gold.
And the Granny Smith
apples just stay green.

The apples aren't ripe yet,
but the kids can't help
climbing the trees to check.

It's late August. Some of the pumpkins have grown as big as basketballs, but they are not quite ready to be picked. They will grow much bigger and turn bright orange.

Mitchell stops by to see his pumpkin again. It's getting bigger still!

As September arrives, the kids go back to school. The days are shorter, and the weather is colder. Lisa visits the orchard with baby Jessica.

Scott brings the boys to the field at the end of the day. He tells Mitchell excitedly, "Go take a look at your pumpkin."

"It's ready!" Mitchell cries as he stands on it in triumph. "It's bigger than I am!" Then he and Kyle try to move the big pumpkin.

Staymen Winesap
Rome Beauty

Pumpkins

←

PICKING TODAY
PUMPKINS
APPLES

←

Red & Golden
Delicious

↑

Up the Hill
to the White House

In October, Scott Applegate and his family look on
with pride as friends and neighbors come to their farm
to pick the beautiful apples and pumpkins.

They watch as
hundreds of
visitors spend
golden
afternoons
filling buckets
with the ripe
apples and
carrying the
pumpkins from
the field.

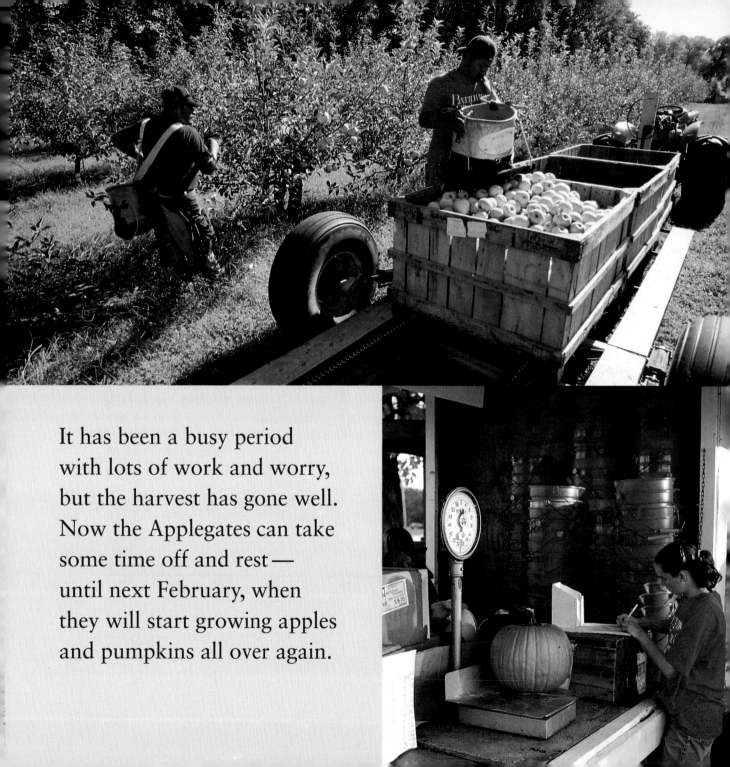

It has been a busy period with lots of work and worry, but the harvest has gone well. Now the Applegates can take some time off and rest—until next February, when they will start growing apples and pumpkins all over again.